DIG IT!
BURIED TREASURE

S.K. Dunn

SCHOLASTIC

DIG IT!

BURIED TREASURE

Written by S.K. Dunn
Illustrated by Daniel Jankowski
Designed by Bill Henderson

Tangerine Press

an imprint of
■ SCHOLASTIC
www.scholastic.com

Scholastic and Tangerine Press and associated logos are trademarks of Scholastic Inc.
Published by Tangerine Press, an imprint of Scholastic Inc., 557 Broadway; New York, NY 10012

Scholastic Canada Ltd.
Markham, Ontario

Scholastic Australia Pty. Ltd
Gosford NSW

Scholastic New Zealand Ltd.
Greenmount, Auckland

Scholastic UK
Coventry, Warwickshire

10 9 8 7 6 5 4 3 2 1

ISBN-10: 0-545-05253-X

ISBN-13: 978-0-545-05253-5

Made in China

Contents

THE FABULOUS WORLD OF THE LOST AND FOUND

Have you ever seen an amazing treasure in a museum and wondered where it came from and who could've found it?

If learning all about treasures is your cup of tea, you've come to the right place! In this book, you'll discover how and why the pursuit of treasure has inspired incredible journeys for thousands of years. You'll learn all about looking for treasures, and how some got lost in the first place. Find out about scientists who seek lost treasures to unlock the secrets of the past and folks who chase after the dream of striking it rich. Some are good guys, and some are bad!

Learn about famous treasures and the folks who found them in unlikely places: from the sealed tomb of an Egyptian king filled with gold and jewels, to golden nuggets plucked by chance from a stream, to pirates' gold and pearls dredged up from deep below the sea.

But the pursuit of treasure isn't just for scientists and swashbucklers of the past. Believe it or not, your own imagination can lead you to amazing discoveries! In this book, you'll find activities and games for drawing a treasure map, making a mini-museum, planning a scavenger hunt, and more!

Then, practice some real hands-on excavation with your own buried treasure by digging out the block that comes with your kit. Finally, play a game of fame and fortune, just like a real treasure hunter.

DIG IN!

WHAT'S A TREASURE, ANYWAY?

You may be wondering what the big deal is about treasures. Sure, they're nice to look at, but what's the point of spending years searching the world for a pot of gold or a diamond necklace? Here's one way to think of it:

At lunchtime, you hand the cashier some money, and he or she hands you a sandwich. It seems weird if you think about it, because a sandwich can nourish you, and a piece of paper can't really do anything, right?

As you know, those "pieces of paper" are money and they're traded for lots of things, not just sandwiches! What they represent is actually the ability to get other things you need. Before people decided on a system of money, or currency, they'd trade valuable items to get what they needed. The things they'd trade were often beautiful and hard to find, such as gold, silver, gems, and pearls. Soon, folks wanted to have rare and pretty things to trade. Having even a few of these things was cool—and having a lot was even better!

Today, people measure their fortunes both with money and precious items. It's a lot easier to carry around bills and coins (and even credit cards!) than it is to lug around all the things you could trade for a sandwich, right?

Thinking about treasures the same way we think of money today can explain why getting and keeping this stuff was, and still is, pretty important to people.

HOW COULD SOMEONE LOSE THAT STUFF?

Ever wonder how valuable stashes of gold and jewels could just be lost? It would only make sense that whoever was lucky enough to own such a fortune in the first place would take pretty good care of it, right?

Here are a few ways that someone's lost stuff can become someone else's treasure.

Gifts to the Gods

Civilizations like the ancient Egyptians and Chinese would bury their dead in big vaults called tombs. Inside the tombs, they would put gold, jewels, and many treasures that they believed the dead person would need in the afterlife. The tombs would be sealed to protect against grave robbers—and were often forgotten about until they're rediscovered.

Hidden Away

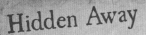

Yet another way that items get lost is by someone hiding them away, planning to come back and get them later. But, like a squirrel burying a nut, sometimes the owners don't come back to get the hidden stash, and it turns into a lucky find for someone else.

Gone but Not Forgotten

Sometimes, people have to leave where they live in a hurry. Maybe a storm is coming. Maybe there's a war. Or maybe they just don't have time to plan a way to get all of their belongings from one place to another in a hurry. The end result of a quick getaway is often a trail of valuables left behind.

Weather or Not

People aren't always an equal match to the forces of Mother Nature. Powerful storms and other natural disasters can often claim cherished items and bury them, either under a pile of mud or below the sea.

WIDE WORLD OF DISCOVERY

Before you read on to find out about some famous treasures—both real and legendary—check this map to see what important fortunes have been found all around the world!

CALIFORNIA
GOLD RUSH
X

USA
CAPTAIN KIDD
X

LOS

X
ANDES MOUNTAINS
EL DORADO

1··2··3··4··5

F POMPEII

X
EGYPT
NG TUT

DIGGIN' FOR A LIVIN'

Hoping to cash in on big money is one reason to go searching for treasure, but there's another reason to look for lost valuables: things that civilizations valued in the past can give us a lot of info on how they lived.

Archaeologists are scientists who hunt treasure. They go looking for lost treasures to figure out how people lived way back in the past. They look to find out about ancient or even lost cultures through skeletal remains, fossils, and objects of human workmanship, like tools, household goods, and even toys.

Archaeologists work on sites called digs to reveal how people lived in the past. Getting through the dirt is a great way to get the dirt on past civilizations and dig up new historical information.

As tempting as it can be, a good archaeologist would never take an artifact for his or her own personal use. To them, the true value of fabulous riches and magnificent discoveries are the secrets to the past that they reveal.

WHAT A DUMP!

As weird or gross as it sounds, archaeologists love a trash heap! A trash heap from a distant culture, called a "midden," can give clues about the kinds of food people ate, the clothes they wore, and even the things they did for fun.

Think about some of the things that you threw away just yesterday—maybe an apple core, an old birthday card, a pair of worn soccer cleats, or some old homework assignments.

AN ARCHAEOLOGIST WHO FOUND YOUR TRASH COULD TELL THAT YOU:

* had a healthy diet and access to fresh fruit (and probably had teeth strong enough to chew).

* lived in a culture that celebrated with rituals like gift giving.

* had enough time for recreational activities.

* lived in a climate where you could play outdoors.

* could read and write, so your culture had language.

Wow! That's a lot of historical information from just one bag of trash!

For archaeologists, the treasure of history is worth more than gold, and the trash of yesterday is today's treasure.

Tools of the Trade

Archaeologists use lots of tools to unearth the treasures of the past. Here are just a few:

TROWEL

Used to slowly remove dirt while excavating to see anything new that may appear in the soil.

MEASURING DEVICES

To measure distances and objects.

NOTEBOOKS AND PENCILS

For recording information about their findings.

MAPS AND CHARTS

To know where to start the dig.

SPOONS

For digging very small, delicate areas.

WHEELBARROW

For moving dirt from the dig site.

And the most important thing that a good archaeologist needs is...old-fashioned hard work!

Looking for lost treasures requires lots of perseverance and patience. As you will see in the following pages, it can take many years for archaeologists to complete their work on projects. But the important discoveries are well worth the effort!

ROOT CLIPPERS AND SAWS

To remove tree roots that may have grown around the dig site.

BRUSHES

To clear dirt from objects.

BIG DIGS!

Archaeologists have made some major discoveries throughout history.

LOST CITY OF POMPEII

The Roman city of Pompeii was a busy vacation spot for citizens of the Roman Empire, full of hustle and bustle—until August 24, A.D. 79, when Mount Vesuvius erupted without warning. The entire town was covered with almost 13 feet (4 m) of volcanic ash and poisonous gas, which smothered all signs of life.

The town was preserved in a near-perfect state, frozen within layers of solidified mud and ash. Since 1748 archaeologists have been digging to reveal Pompeii's secrets. The discoveries include room-size paintings called frescoes, marble and bronze sculptures, jewelry, gold coins, and everyday household items, which give us a true picture of life during the Roman era.

THE BOSCOREALE TREASURE

Another town that suffered the effects of Mount Vesuvius was the nearby village of Boscoreale.

In 1895, a man named Vincenzo de Prisco discovered a fabulous collection of gold and silver stashed away in a cistern, most likely to protect it from the eruption. The collection contained gold coins and jewelry, as well as 109 pieces of ornately designed silverware, including bowls, cups, and plates. Aside from the riches of de Prisco's

find, the intricate details on the dishes offer an excellent example of Roman metalwork from the first century A.D.

Today, most of what is known as the Boscoreale Treasure can be seen in the Louvre Museum in Paris, France.

Many of the artifacts found in Pompeii are exhibited in museums around the world today, including the Naples Museum of Archaeology in Italy.

KING TUT

In 1922, British archaeologist Howard Carter uncovered a sealed tomb in Egypt that was revealed to be that of King Tutankhamun. The young king, or pharaoh, commonly known as King Tut to us now, was only 9 years old when he began his reign in 1334 B.C. He is believed to have died around his 18th or 19th birthday.

As short as his reign was, the riches of tribute to King Tut were spectacular—in all, some 3,500 items were recovered. Within the tomb, Carter discovered a spectacular array of fantastic treasures, including the boy-king's solid gold funeral mask, lamps, jars, jewelry, furniture, and other precious objects that the ancient Egyptians believed the young king would need for the afterlife. Even the young pharaoh's coffin was made of solid gold!

From 1976 to 1979, a smaller number of treasures from Tutankhamun's tomb were displayed in the United States during a seven-city tour of "Treasures of Tutankhamun," which attracted eight million visitors and set traveling show attendance records—making it the most popular museum exhibition of all time!

Because of the tour's popularity with crowds, a second exhibition was organized and brought to Philadelphia, Pennsylvania, in February 2007 through September 2007. The exhibition includes approximately 130 objects from the tomb of King Tut and other Valley of the King ancestors.

Look Out Below!

With about 70 percent of the planet covered in ocean, it seems only logical that under the sea would be a pretty good place to look for buried treasure.

Nautical Archaeologists

Nautical archaeologists, like their counterparts on dry land, use many different tools to locate and excavate underwater sites. Because it's not possible to see everything at the bottom of the ocean unless you're a fish, nautical archaeologists rely on sonar to do the "looking" for them. Sonar works by throwing out sound energy and measuring the strength of the return signal that bounces back off the seafloor or other large, submerged items. The patterns that emerge create a kind of map of the area below. This is basically the same "tool" used by a bat to navigate its way through caves.

One of the most important tools used in underwater excavation is sidescan sonar. Sidescan sonar is used by all kinds of underwater searchers including law enforcement agencies, military units, and dive rescue groups.

Other Tools Used To

Scuba diving equipment
Allows divers to breathe underwater so can they search for longer periods of time.

Fortune Seekers

Another group that uses sidescan sonar is marine salvage companies. Marine salvage companies look for remains of ships in the hopes of making profits by either selling the wreckage cargo and artifacts to museums, or by presenting exhibits of the recovered treasures.

"Cargo sales" refer to items, or cargo, found on a ship that are not considered culturally significant. For example, if a shipwreck was found with a large cargo of gold coins, a marine salvager might sell some of those coins, after documenting, studying, and setting aside a representative sample for future study and exhibition.

FIND SUNKEN GOODS:

Remotely operated vehicles (ROVs)

Little robots equipped with cameras that can travel places too difficult for humans to go.

Water dredge and airlift

Like an underwater vacuum cleaner, these tools suck up debris to be examined above the water's surface.

Metal detectors

Excellent for locating things like coins, cannons, and even nails from a submerged ship's hull.

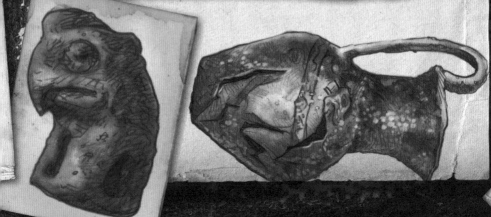

SHIPWRECKS

Throughout history, people have used ships to transport themselves and their belongings across oceans. A sad reality of life on the sea is that it can be unpredictable, especially when weather is involved. Huge storms at sea called tropical cyclones could topple an enormous ship and all of its contents,

sending it crashing to the bottom of the ocean—often never to be seen again.

While the loss is devastating, sunken treasures of lost ships are a tempting lure for adventurers and fortune hunters. Modern technology and knowing where to search have landed big payoffs for some lucky fortune hunters.

THE *SANTA MARGARITA*

Time and patience can be invaluable when it comes to looking for treasure. In 1622, the *Santa Margarita*, a treasure ship destined for Spain with riches from the New World, was sunk during a terrible hurricane. The severe storm doomed the *Santa Margarita* and her crew and cargo to the bottom of the sea for more than 200 years. Marine salvagers discovered the hull of the ill-fated ship in 1980, but it wasn't until the summer of 2007 when the valuable cargo was retrieved by a team of divers off the coast of the Florida Keys.

The initial haul revealed a gold bar, eight gold chains, and 11 ornate gold pieces. Later, divers dragged 17 tons (20 tonnes) of gold and silver coins from this wreck. And later still, divers recovered an even rarer treasure: a sealed lead box containing thousands of loose pearls! The treasures were found in nearly 18 feet (5.5 m) of water about 40 miles (64 km) west of Key West. Today, the search continues for the rest of the estimated $150 to $200 million (U.S.) of treasure in the still-undiscovered main portion of the shipwreck.

PIRATES

Not all people seeking treasures go about it honestly. A less savory sort of treasure hunter is a pirate. Unlike archaeologists and salvagers, pirates captured ships and their cargos by force.

The Golden Age of Piracy in the Caribbean lasted from the late 17th century until the early 18th century, when riches from the Americas and the Caribbean were sent back to Europe as quickly as they could be gathered. Huge ships loaded with gold, spices, and other precious cargo were tempting targets for pirates.

The adventurous life of a pirate has been made popular in movies and literature as fun and romantic, but the truth is pirates were—and still are— nothing more than robbers at sea. The dangerous work of pirates pitted them not only against the law, but also against each other. It was not uncommon for them to rebel and take over a ship from the pirate captain. A rebellion at sea is called a mutiny.

Not Just for the Boys
While the most famous pirates like Edward Teach, a.k.a. "Blackbeard," and Captain Kidd were men, some women were also drawn into the pirate lifestyle. Two women, Anne Bonny and Mary Read, are famous female pirates who disguised themselves as men.

SPANISH MAIN

From the 16th to 18th centuries, the area known as the Spanish Main was the mainland coast of the Spanish Empire around the Caribbean. The long stretch of coastline owned by Spain included Florida, Mexico, Central America, and the north coast of South America.

Huge ships departed from the Spanish Main destined for Spain with loads of gold, silver, gems, spices, hardwoods, hides, and other prizes from the New World.

The fabulous cargo aboard these ships made the Spanish Main a popular place for pirates looking to score some treasures of their own.

THE LEGEND OF CAPTAIN KIDD'S TREASURE

One of the most famous pirates of all time was Captain Kidd. In 1695, William Kidd was a captain of the British navy working to capture pirates and reclaim their stolen loot for England. But after some months of disappointment with life on the side of good, Kidd turned into one of the very pirates he had hunted.

Captain Kidd traveled with his crew of pirates throughout the West Indies, eventually settling in New York. Pirates like Kidd often traveled between East Hampton and New York City because New York was a good place to sell their treasures. Eventually, Captain Kidd surrendered to authorities and was hanged to death as a pirate in 1701.

Legend has it that Captain Kidd buried his treasure in up to 15 different locations around Long Island. Treasure hunters and historians say his loot is most likely still hidden on Gardiner's Island, Oyster Bay, Sayville, and an inlet near East Hampton. Although no treasure has ever been recovered, rumors continue that a hidden fortune is buried for some lucky treasure hunter.

COMING BY IT NATURALLY

One day in 1848, a man named James Wilson Marshall saw a golden glint in a stream at Sutter's Mill in California. When he retrieved the glittering piece of metal, he did the first thing he knew to test the gold: he bit it. Gold is softer than other metals and chomping teeth should leave a mark—which they did!

Next, Marshall turned to an unlikely source: the mill's cook, Jennie Wilmer. Mrs. Wilmer knew to boil the nugget in a pot of lye soap to test if the gold was real. If it wasn't genuine gold, the metal would react with the lye and turn green. The nugget stayed as gold in Mrs. Wilmer's pot as it had first appeared to Marshall in the stream. Further research from an old encyclopedia combined with Mrs. Wilmer's "cooking" confirmed Marshall's belief.

Although Marshall tried to keep the discovery a secret, word got out. By 1849, hundreds of thousands of people from all around the world were traveling to California in hopes of striking it rich. The California Gold Rush was on!

Early prospectors, called Forty-Niners (from the year 1849 when the most people came), searched for gold in streams and rivers by a simple technique called panning. Although it's believed that most of the richest deposits of gold have been mined out, you can still visit places in California and try your hand at panning for gold!

TOO GOOD TO BE TRUE?

Long before real gold was discovered in California, New World explorers searched for the legendary treasure of the lost city of El Dorado.

The name El Dorado is Spanish, meaning "gilded one" or "gilded man." When Spain conquered the Aztec and Inca empires in the 16th century, Spanish conquistadors heard tales of a fabulous fortune of gold they called El Dorado.

The legend goes that, once a year, a chief covered in gold dust would sail out on a raft into the middle of a mountain lake and make offerings to the gods of gold and other precious things.

Although the conquistadors did find a great deal of precious gold and silver artwork, which they claimed for Spain, the mysterious fortune of El Dorado puzzled treasure seekers for many years. Over time, the legend grew and grew, and El Dorado came to be thought of as an actual city of gold, inspiring many explorers from the 1500s on.

GOLDEN TRUTHS

The beauty of gold has been enough to enchant cultures for centuries—but today we know there's more to gold than meets the eye. Here are some fun facts about gold that you may not know.

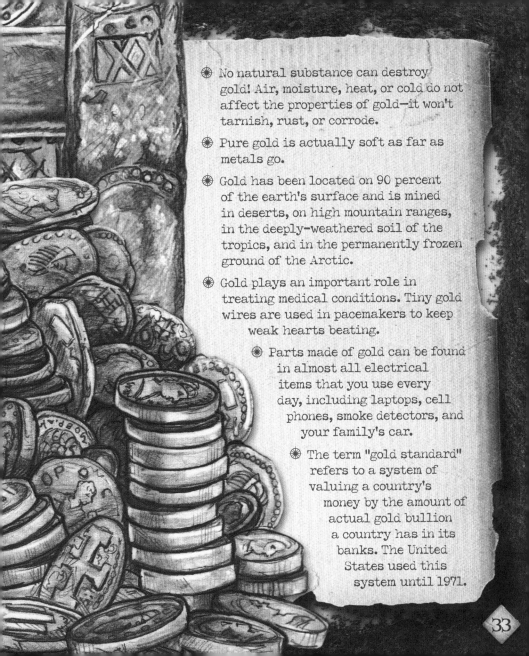

✸ No natural substance can destroy gold! Air, moisture, heat, or cold do not affect the properties of gold—it won't tarnish, rust, or corrode.

✸ Pure gold is actually soft as far as metals go.

✸ Gold has been located on 90 percent of the earth's surface and is mined in deserts, on high mountain ranges, in the deeply-weathered soil of the tropics, and in the permanently frozen ground of the Arctic.

✸ Gold plays an important role in treating medical conditions. Tiny gold wires are used in pacemakers to keep weak hearts beating.

✸ Parts made of gold can be found in almost all electrical items that you use every day, including laptops, cell phones, smoke detectors, and your family's car.

✸ The term "gold standard" refers to a system of valuing a country's money by the amount of actual gold bullion a country has in its banks. The United States used this system until 1971.

YOU CAN DIG IT, TOO!

Remember the time you found a crumpled bill in your pocket that you had been saving to get an ice cream cone? Maybe you thought about it and decided to go through the pockets of all of your shorts, jeans, and tops, looking for other bills and change that you may have stashed and forgotten about, or just plain lost. Well, if you've done that, you've had a mini-treasure hunting experience!

You don't have to be an archaeologist or a pirate to have fun looking for forgotten objects and clues to the past. As you know by now, treasures can be just about anything. Things that may seem ordinary and everyday to you now may have special value to you or somebody else someday.

Exploration and searching the high seas may be way off in your future, but you can hone your seeking skills right now. Check out the following pages for creative ways to begin treasure hunting!

WHAT'S THE BUZZ?

A fun, inexpensive tool you can get for finding buried objects is a metal detector. Where should you look for things with your metal detector? Basically, any place people lose things! Beaches, public parks, playgrounds, and even your own backyard are fun places to find treasure. If you want to have a more adventurous hunting experience, ask an adult to take you hiking in the woods, and bring along your detector to search for some long-forgotten items.

SOME TIPS ABOUT YOUR METAL DETECTOR

* Most metal detectors can find things buried only about one foot (30.5 cm) or so beneath the surface.

* Some metals, like iron, create a stronger magnetic field, making it easier for the detector to pick up a signal.

* The bigger the object, the more detectable it is. In other words, you're more likely to find some lost keys than you are a small coin.

* Finding objects with a metal detector can also depend on where and how long an object has been buried. Certain minerals in soil are natural conductors and can seriously interfere with the metal detector. When certain types of metal objects have been in the ground for a long time, they can actually increase the conductivity of the soil around them. This creates what's called a "halo" around the object.

* Things like underground pipes and cables, or aboveground telephone or power cables can interfere with the detector's signal.

MINI-MUSEUM

Create your own mini-museum by going on an archaeological dig at some place you may visit every day. When you collect specimens and catalog your findings, you just may have a new view of a familiar world!

WHAT YOU DO:

1. Select a space that you are familiar with and go for a walk with a grownup or some friends. If you live near a pond or the ocean, walk along the shore and look for things that have washed up.

2. In a small notebook, write the date and exact location where you found your object. Describe it as best you can, including all of the littlest details. Was it dirty or chipped? Try to describe the shape, color, and size. Was it the only one or were there lots like it?

3. Use a permanent marker to write the date and location of your find on a sticker or a piece of masking tape. Put the sticker or tape on the outside of the jar or section of the egg carton.

4. Keep adding treasures to your mini-museum!

YOU'LL NEED:

⁕ Plastic bags for collecting specimens
⁕ A small notebook
⁕ A pen or pencil
⁕ A permanent marker
⁕ Stickers or masking tape
⁕ An old egg carton or small jars

Locket

Shell

Necklace

KEEP ON DIGGING

Learn more about the location where you found your treasures. For example, if you found a lot of quartz rocks in your backyard, do a little research on rocks in your part of the country. Your findings could lead to all sorts of new discoveries!

Rocks!

Starfish

BACKYARD TREASURE HUNT

Try to think like a pirate or someone planning a quick escape. Where would you stash away your favorite goods? Your backyard? A favorite playground? Maybe you've got a secret spot that only you and your best bud know about. Being able to find your treasure is just as important as hiding it. Think of Captain Kidd not being able to find all of his lost treasure!

Try this cool activity to test your treasure hiding-and-seeking skills.

YOU'LL NEED:

* An object to hide
* A plain piece of paper
* Crayons
* A piece of twine or ribbon
* A clean, empty bottle (optional)

SOME DECORATING TIPS:

Use crayons to draw the map– ink may run and pencil may smudge or be too light.

Tear the edges of the paper to make it look ragged and worn.

Brush a thin layer of vegetable oil over the map or spray on some nonstick cooking spray, then quickly blot it off with a paper towel. It'll make plain paper look like parchment paper from the olden days.

WHAT YOU DO:

1. Select an object to hide, like a coin, a small toy, a box, or even a note placed in a plastic sandwich bag.

2. Draw a map of the territory. Include landmarks to make the boundaries clear for the seekers, such as the biggest tree, the doghouse, the grill, your bed, and the house. Be as detailed as you can.

3. Find a good hiding spot within that territory. You don't have to bury it—but if you do, be sure to ask before you dig! Mark the hiding spot with a big **X** on your map.

4. Starting at the hiding spot, count off paces to one of the landmarks you drew. Write the number of steps you took on the map. Repeat this from the other landmarks.

5. Write directions to go with the map, such as, "Start at the willow tree and walk 32 paces west." Since you may not have a compass, make the directions detailed.

6. To make your map look authentic, carefully crumple it into a ball, then smooth it out and roll it into a scroll. Tie it with a piece of twine or a ribbon, or slip it into a bottle. (Just make sure the map slips back out easily or you've just wasted a lot of effort.)

7. Invite someone to find the hidden treasure. No helping! Your map and written directions should be the only clues to discovering your hidden treasure.

GO ON A SCAVENGER HUNT

Sometimes, treasure hunters don't have a map to guide them. They just hear about an object, whether legendary or real, and set out to find it on their own.

A scavenger hunt is a fun way to rely on your skills of knowing where to look and how.

YOU'LL NEED:

- ✳ 2 or more players
- ✳ A list of items to discover
- ✳ A watch for each member of the team

WHAT YOU DO:

1. Divide into teams. The more players, the more fun—it's best to have at least two people per team.

2. Set a boundary for the hunt. It can be as small as your bedroom or as big as your whole neighborhood, but everyone needs to agree on the territory of the hunt to make things fair.

3. Agree on a time that the hunt will begin and end. The time limit is very important! It provides the biggest challenge and gives everyone an equal chance. Make sure that everyone on the teams has a watch to keep track of the time.

4. Ask an adult to come up with a list of objects to find, or use the suggestions listed below. Distribute a copy of the list to each of the teams, and you're off!

The first team to get all of the objects on the list before the time is up wins!

SOME SUGGESTIONS FOR YOUR LIST:

❋ A picture of a ship

❋ A feather

❋ Something soft

❋ Something shiny

❋ Something that fits in your pocket

❋ Something you are too old to play with

❋ Something purple

UNEARTHING YOUR TREASURE

Your kit comes with a digging block for you to practice excavating a treasure of your own, as well as a digging tool, and a brush. Follow these simple steps to reveal your treasure, and then compare your discovery with the pictures on the following page to determine what you have.

Be sure to change into an old T-shirt before you start the excavation. Things could get messy!

YOU'LL NEED:

* A large sheet of white paper or newspaper
* Digging block from your kit
* Digging tool from your kit
* Brush from your kit

WHAT YOU DO:

1. Spread the paper out on a flat surface, and place the block in the center of the paper.

2. Using the digging tool, gently scrape away the clay. When you see an object through the clay, dig around it very carefully.

3. Remove all the clay from the object before you take it out of the block.

4. Keep digging until you've scraped away all of the clay and you're left with your new treasure. Gently brush it to get rid of any extra clay.

If you need to, wash off any remaining clay from your treasure with water to really make it sparkle!

ROMAN COIN

JADE

ROSE QUARTZ

AMETHYST

PERIDOT

Fame or Fortune?

A Card Game for Two Players

As you know by now, the two biggest payoffs in looking for treasure are fame and fortune. Folks like archaeologists aren't really looking to cash in on big money as much as they're looking to make a new discovery for a museum. But other kinds of treasure hunters are out there looking for the big bucks!

Here's a game you and a friend can play to try your hand at a little bit of digging without getting dirty—or even leaving the house!

DIG IT!
BURIED
TREASUR

FAME
OR
FORTUNE?

FAME
100 POINTS
FORTUNE
0 POINTS

FAME
0 PO
FORTU
100 P

FAME
100 POINTS
FORTUNE
0 POINTS

SILVER
GOBLET

In your
grandmother's
attic, you

YOU'LL NEED:

1. Playing cards from your kit
2. Scorecard (found on p. 48)
3. Pencil

FAME · O POINTS

FORTUNE · 100 POINTS

BRONZE STATUE
You find a sm...
a seaho...

HOW TO PLAY

1. Before the game starts, flip a coin to determine who goes first. The player who goes first decides whether he or she wants to play for Fame or Fortune.

2. Write down whether you're going for "Fame" or "Fortune" on the scorecard in the back of your book.

3. Shuffle all the cards and lay them facedown.

4. Take turns flipping over two cards to get a matching pair. If you don't get a match, flip the cards back over, and it's your opponent's turn.

5. If the cards match up, you earn 100 points for your category. For example, if you are playing for Fame, you must flip over a matching pair that says, "Fame 100 Points". If you match up your opponent's cards, you can take these from the playing field—but neither of you will earn points.

6. Once a pair has been matched up, remove them from the playing field.

7. Keep track of your scores on the scorecard. Keep playing until all of the cards have been matched.

8. Add up your points. The player who earns the most points wins. If it's a tie, play again!

SCORECARD

	Player 1	Player 2
	Fortune Matt	Fame Mom
Round 1	1200	500
Round 2		200
Round 3		600
TOTAL		1800

	Player 1	Player 2
Round 1		
Round 2		
Round 3		
TOTAL		

	Player 1	Player 2
Round 1		
Round 2		
Round 3		
TOTAL		

	Player 1	Player 2
Round 1		
Round 2		
Round 3		
TOTAL		

	Player 1	Player 2
Round 1		
Round 2		
Round 3		
TOTAL		

	Player 1	Player 2
Round 1		
Round 2		
Round 3		
TOTAL		